1050

North Star
ST HERMAN OF ALASKA

Dorrie Papademetriou

ST VLADIMIR'S SEMINARY PRESS

LIBRARY OF CONGRESS
CATALOGING-IN-PUBLCATION DATA

Papademetriou, Dorrie, 1963-
North Star: St. Herman of Alaska / Dorrie
Papademetriou
    p. cm.
ISBN 0-88141-223-6
    1. German Aëiskinskåæ, Saint, 1756-1837—
Juvenile literature. 2. Missionaries—Alaska—Spruce
Island—Biography—Juvenile literature. 3. Russkaëi
pravoslavnaëi ëierkov§'-Alaska—Spruce Island—
Clergy—Biography—Juvenile literature. 4. Aleuts—
Missions—History—Juvenile literature. [1. Herman,
of Alaska, Saint, 1756-1837. 2. Saints. 3. Missionaries.
4. Aleuts. 5. Indians of North America—Alaska.
6. Spruce Island (Alaska)] I. Title.

BX597.G47 P36 2000
281.9'092—dc 21
                                    00-051786

For Peter

*A special thank you to Tom, George,
and Roman for your love of history
and curiosity which inspired me to
write this book.*

*The publication of this book
was made possible through a gift
made in the memory of
Mrs. Sophie Koulomzin (†2000),
author, teacher and pioneer in
Orthodox Christian education.*

NORTH STAR
Saint Herman of Alaska

St Vladimir's Seminary Press
575 Scarsdale Rd.
Crestwood, NY 10707
1-800-204-2665

Copyright © 2001
by Dorrie Papademetriou

ISBN 0-88141-223-6

PRINTED IN HONG KONG

HISTORICAL NOTE

In 1794, a group of ten Orthodox Christian missionaries from Russia reached Alaska.

It was an unusually long journey, taking a year to traverse 7,900 miles by land and sea. Father Herman was one of the men to arrive at Kodiak Island. From there Father Herman went to live on the smaller Spruce Island. He lived there for more than forty years and worked on behalf of and prayed for the natives until his death in 1836. On August 9, 1970 he was proclaimed a saint and is known throughout the world as "Saint Herman of Alaska."

Hymns to St Herman

O Blessed Father Herman of Alaska,
North Star of Christ's Holy Church.
The light of your Holy life and great deeds
guides those who follow the Orthodox way.
Together we lift high the Holy Cross you
planted firmly in America.
Let all behold and glorify Jesus Christ,
singing His Holy Resurrection.

～

The eternal light of
Christ our Savior guided you,
O blessed Father Herman,
on your journey to America.
Now you stand before the Lord of glory,
interceding for your new land
and its people,
praying ceaselessly for the
salvation of our souls.

On wintry nights I walk through the snow-carpeted forest of my home on Spruce Island. I feel the silvery moon peer over my shoulder when I look to the North Star. The North Star is always just above me because I live in Alaska. With wonder and admiration, I remember.

For me, and for all of my Aleut brothers and sisters, Father Herman is our North Star. He lights up the sky with his golden rays of goodness. He makes sure we follow our true path.

He is the man we called "Apa," which in our language means "grandfather."

Let me tell you how I first met Apa. One day, many years ago, I stood at the edge of the forest on my island. I looked out at the mighty sea and saw a small boat coming through the mist. The deep blue rolling waves tossed it about, up and down, up and down, up and down. The boat carried one single man, a man I did not yet know.

He was a man from Russia, a land that lies far across the vast ocean from Alaska. At first he came with nine of his friends and settled on Kodiak Island, which is just a few miles from my own island. There he and his friends built wooden homes. They became friends with the natives of Kodiak and began to teach them about God.

It was terribly sad that most of these men drowned in a ship-wreck. After a time, only this one man remained.

He first came across the dangerous northern ocean to our craggy, mountainous seashore. He came to this quiet wilderness to live on Spruce Island. He made his simple home in the middle of the emerald forest. Here among the towering spruce trees he prayed to Jesus. He sent his prayers straight up to heaven.

Apa was a small, but very strong, man. I watched as he cleared the rugged land by himself. One time, I saw him carry a heavy log—a log as big as a canoe, a log that would be too heavy for three, or even four, men to carry. But Father Herman lifted that log all by himself, and he did it barefooted!

Why was he so strong? The secret, Apa said, was that God's Spirit inside of him made him very, very strong.

For a house, Father Herman dug himself a hut called a *barabara*. It was a space carved into the ground and covered with sod. My own native people had lived in these kinds of houses for hundreds of years.

But Apa was *not* like my people in many ways. He had a flat stone for a bed! He had two rocks covered with animal skins for pillows! He ate very little food. He spent his days working and praying.

Everyone from miles around could recognize him. He was the man with the long flowing hair and bushy beard that turned whiter with each passing year.

He wore a large deerskin tunic. Over time this leather tunic became so worn that it glistened and shone like the sun. On the outside he wore a long black robe that was patched in many places.

His skin was lighter than mine, and his language different from mine. But when I first met him, his pleasant smile and bluish gray sparkling eyes made me feel like I was already his friend.

Even though Father Herman didn't eat much himself, he knew how to cook and how to grow and prepare food so that there was enough for my people to eat. He boiled the salt out of ocean water and used it to preserve our food for the winter season. He gathered huge baskets of seaweed and showed us Aleuts how to fertilize our gardens.

Because the sun doesn't set in Alaska during the summer months, our vegetables and fruits grow to enormous sizes. Cabbages usually look like small boulders. But with Apa's help, it seemed they grew as big as the midnight sun!

Spruce Island is full of creatures of every size and shape. Apa loved them all. The playful sea otters frolicked on the shore when he came near. The shy fox would creep out from his den to sneak a peek at him as he tended his garden.

Once I saw a ferocious Kodiak bear approach Father Herman. Instead of being afraid, Apa walked right over to the hungry bear and fed him a fish for supper! Standing on its hind legs, that bear was twice as tall as my friend was. But the bear ate the fish right out of Apa's hand, as if they, too, were lifelong friends.

Father Herman especially loved children, and there were many little children in my village. He baked lots of cookies and biscuits, called *kredilki*, for us.

We gathered close around him. With his sparkling eyes and sweet voice, he told us stories of far away places. He told us how God loved us. And he told us we should love God. "From this day, from this hour, from this very minute, we should love God above all and fulfill His holy will." He built a school for us and taught us songs and prayers. As we sang, the spruce trees around us swayed gently to the sound of our soft voices.

Father Herman was our protector. Other men from across the ocean had come to Alaska to hunt and trap wild animals and sell their fur. They called themselves "traders." Some were kind, like Apa. They became part of our families. But some were cruel. They came to take gold from the earth. They wasted the land and its natural resources. They almost destroyed the largest herd of seals in the world. They made us work for little or no money.

Apa often met with the leaders of the traders to beg them to treat our people kindly. He told them, "Our Creator granted the native Aleut people this homeland." He wrote letters to governors and church leaders, asking them to stop the harmful traders from hurting our country and us. Apa was our hero.

Winters in Alaska are very harsh and cold and dark. This is the season when the sun hides itself for most of the day. Everything becomes silent under a blanket of snow.

One winter was unusually harsh. Many of my people became terribly sick. We had no doctor and no medicine. Illness spread rapidly through our village, and many people died. Small children and babies were especially in danger. My little sister became sick, and I expected the worst to happen. Then Apa came to her with his soothing smile. He cared for her and others. He brought food and warm blankets to our home. He comforted us with his warm spirit as he told stories by our bedsides.

For a whole month he cared for the village folk, never tiring and always praying. He stayed with us until the sickness passed. My sister became well again. How could I ever repay my dear Father Herman? I had no money, or anything of value to give him. Then I had an idea.

I saw Father Herman standing
alone under the star-filled
winter sky. He stood watching
the northern lights as bright
as a rainbow. Ribbons of
yellow, pink, and green
filled the sky.

I walked over to him,
and set my hand in his.
"Apa," I said, "I made this
for you. Thank you for
saving my sister. Without
you, we would have
suffered from the cold and
starved, and the sickness
would have taken us away to
the land of the dead."

He looked down at the small
wooden whale I had carved from a
piece of island driftwood. He closed
his fingers around my gift and held it to
his heart. "Thank you," he said to me.
Then we both turned to gaze into the bright
sky, feeling its warmth and beauty.

Father Herman quietly began to sing one of our church
hymns, "O Joyous Light of the Holy Glory…" He knew God was
listening. And so did I.

Once, a frightening fire raged through the forest on Spruce Island. It threatened to destroy my village. Quickly, Father Herman dug a ditch about three feet wide next to a thicket in the forest. We worked together and turned over moss all the way to the bottom of the hill near the village. Completely exhausted, Apa turned to me and said, "Rest assured, the fire will not pass this line."

The next day looked very grim. Billowing clouds filled the sky with black smoke, and a gusting wind pushed the blazing fire toward us. My eyes stung from the smoke. I was so afraid, I couldn't even move.

Then, when the fire reached the place where we had overturned the earth, it suddenly halted.

The thick
forest
beyond
remained untouched.
My village was safe.

Father Herman saved our village another time—
an even scarier time. A powerful tidal wave came out of
the deep ocean and shook Spruce Island. The mighty sea
roared loudly, and great crashing waves raced to the
shore. My people ran in all directions, trying to escape
the storm. They fled to higher ground, but I ran to Apa.
Quickly, Father Herman took an icon of the Virgin Mary
and ran to the shore. He placed the icon firmly in the
sand and began to pray.

He calmly turned to me and said, "Have no fear. The
water will go no higher than where this holy icon
stands." But the waters still rolled thunderously. We were
all terrified. As the waves came closer and were about to
crash onto the shore, they suddenly stopped in midair.
They became calm and lapped onto the sand where the
icon stood.

Our fear turned to amazement. We smiled at the
wondrous miracle. We fell to our knees and wept in
relief. We thanked God, and our dear Father Herman.
Thanks to Apa's prayers, our homes were safe again.

In the evenings, by the firelight, we gathered around Father Herman. We told each other stories about our ancestors, our grandmothers and grandfathers, and great-grandmothers and great-grandfathers. He told us about God's love, about heaven, about eternity, and about the saint heroes that we all loved to hear about. We talked and listened well past midnight, into the early morning hours.

I once asked Apa, "How do you manage to live alone in the forest? Don't you ever get lonesome?" He answered smiling, "But, I am *not* alone! God is there, as He is everywhere. Holy angels are there. With whom is it better and more pleasant to talk, with men or with angels? Of course, with angels!"

I curled up under my mother's blanket. I pretended I was under angels' wings and drifted off to sleep.

Year after year, as I grew up, I understood more and more about Father Herman. I knew him as a friend, as my ever-shining North Star, my guide. He brought the message of God's love to my village. He filled our hearts with God's love. He listened to us and protected us, the Aleuts of Spruce Island, the Aleuts of this great land called America.

One evening, we saw an unusual pillar of light flowing upward from our island into the night sky. Never before had we seen such an amazing sight. It was as if a huge, bright candle stretched its warm flame up to heaven. One of our wise old men said, "Father Herman has left us," and he began to pray. A warm feeling came over us all. Through the darkness we gazed at the brilliant light filling the world.

And the words of Apa came back to my ears, "From this day, from this hour, from this very minute, we should love God above all and fulfill His holy will."

The North Star is always above me
because I live in Alaska.
Father Herman is *our* North Star,
forever guiding us in God's way.